Environ rich Europa to the north;
All fetch'd
From out your courts by beauty to this coast
To seek and sue for fair Angelica;
Sith none but one must have this happy prize
At which you all have levell'd long your thoughts,
Set each man forth his passions how he can,
And let her censure make the happiest man.

SOLDAN

The fairest flower that glories Africa,
Whose beauty Phœbus dares not dash with showers,
Over whose climate never hung a cloud,
But smiling Titan lights the horizon,—
Egypt is mine, and there I hold my state,
Seated in Cairo and in Babylon.
From thence the matchless beauty of Angelica,
Whose hue's as bright as are those silver doves
That wanton Venus mann'th upon her fist,
Forc'd me to cross and cut th' Atlantic seas,
To oversearch the fearful ocean,
Where I arriv'd t' eternize with my lance
The matchless beauty of fair Angelica;
Nor tilt, nor tourney, but my spear and shield
Resounding on their crests and sturdy helms,
Topt high with plumes, like Mars his burgonet,
Enchasing on their curats with my blade,
That none so fair as fair Angelica.
But leaving these such glories as they be,
I love, my lord; let that suffice for me.

RODOMONT

Cuba my seat, a region so enrich'd
With favours sparkling from the smiling heavens,
As those that seek for traffic to my coast
Account it like that wealthy Paradise
From whence floweth Gihon and swift Euphrates:
The earth within her bowels hath enwrapt,
As in the massy storehouse of the world,
Millions of gold, as bright as was the shower
That wanton Jove sent down to Danäe.
Marching from thence to manage arms abroad,
I pass'd the triple-parted regiment
That froward Saturn gave unto his sons,
Erecting statues of my chivalry,
Such and so brave as never Hercules
Vow'd for the love of lovely Iole.
But leaving these such glories as they be,

I love, my lord; let that suffice for me.

MANDRICARD
And I, my lord, am Mandricard of Mexico,
Whose climate's fairer than Iberia's,
Seated beyond the sea of Tripoly,
And richer than the plot Hesperides,
Or that same isle wherein Ulysses' love
Lull'd in her lap the young Telegonus;
That did but Venus tread a dainty step,
So would she like the land of Mexico,
As, Paphos and brave Cyprus set aside,
With me sweet lovely Venus would abide.
From thence, mounted upon a Spanish bark,
Such as transported Jason to the fleece,
Come from the south, I furrow'd Neptune's seas,
Northeast as far as is the frozen Rhene;
Leaving fair Voya, cross'd up Danuby,
As high as Saba, whose enhancing streams
Cut 'twixt the Tartars and the Russians:
There did I act as many brave attempts,
As did Pirithöus for his Proserpine.
But leaving these such glories as they be,
I love, my lord; let that suffice for me.

BRANDIMART
The bordering islands, seated herein ken,
Whose shores are sprinkled with rich orient pearl,
More bright of hue than were the margarites
That Cæsar found in wealthy Albion;
The sands of Tagus all of burnish'd gold
Made Thetis never prouder on the clifts
That overpeer the bright and golden shore,
Than do the rubbish of my country seas:
And what I dare, let say the Portingale,
And Spaniard tell, who, mann'd with mighty fleets,
Came to subdue my islands to their king,
Filling our seas with stately argosies,
Calvars and magars, hulks of burden great;
Which Brandimart rebated from his coast,
And sent them home ballass'd with little wealth.
But leaving these such glories as they be,
I love, my lord; let that suffice for me.

ORLANDO
Lords of the south, and princes of esteem,
Viceroys unto the state of Africa,
I am no king, yet am I princely born,

The History of Orlando Furioso by Robert Greene

Robert Greene was, by the best accounts available, born in Norwich in 1558 and baptised on July 11th.

Greene is believed to have been a pupil at Norwich Grammar School and then attended Cambridge receiving his B.A. in 1580, and an M.A. in 1583. He then moved to London and began an extraordinary chapter in his life as a widely published author.

His literary career began with the publication of the long romance, 'Mamillia', (1580). Greene's romances were written in a highly wrought style which reached its peak in 'Pandosto' (1588) and 'Menaphon' (1589). Short poems and songs incorporated in some of the romances attest to his ability as a lyric poet.

In 1588, he was granted an MA from Oxford University, almost certainly as a courtesy degree. Thereafter he sometimes placed the phrase Utruisq. Academiae in Artibus Magister', "Master of Arts in both Universities" on the title page of his works.

The lack of records hinders any complete biography of Greene but he did write an autobiography of sorts, but where the balance lies between facts and artistic licence is not clearly drawn. According to that autobiography 'The Repentance of Robert Greene', Greene is alleged to have written 'A Groatsworth of Wit Bought with a Million of Repentance' during the month prior to his death, including in it a letter to his wife asking her to forgive him and stating that he was sending their son back to her.

His output was prolific. Between 1583 and 1592, he published more than twenty-five works in prose, becoming one of the first authors in England to support himself with his pen in an era when professional authorship was virtually unknown.

In his 'coney-catching' pamphlets, Greene fashioned himself into a well-known public figure, narrating colourful inside stories of rakes and rascals duping young gentlemen and solid citizens out of their hard-earned money. These stories, told from the perspective of a repentant former rascal, have been considered autobiographical, and to incorporate many facts of Greene's own life thinly veiled as fiction. However, the alternate account suggests that Greene invented almost everything, merely displaying his undoubted skills as a writer.

In addition to his prose works, Greene also wrote several plays, none of them published in his lifetime, including 'The Scottish History of James IV', 'Alphonsus', and his greatest popular success, 'Friar Bacon and Friar Bungay', as well as 'Orlando Furioso', based on Ludovico Ariosto's Orlando Furioso.

His plays earned himself the title as one of the 'University Wits', a group that included George Peele, Thomas Nashe, and Christopher Marlowe.

Robert Greene died 3rd September 1592.

Index of Contents
DRAMATIS PERSONÆ

THE HISTORY OF ORLANDO FURIOSO
ROBERT GREENE - A SHORT BIOGRAPHY
ROBERT GREENE - A CONCISE BIBLIOGRAPHY

DRAMATIS PERSONÆ
MARSILIUS, Emperor of Africa
SOLDAN OF EGYPT
RODOMONT, King of Cuba
MANDRICARD, King of Mexico
BRANDIMART, King of the Isles
SACRIPANT
ORLANDO
OGIER
NAMUS
OLIVER
TURPIN
DUKE OF AQUITAIN
ROSSILION
MEDOR
ORGALIO, page to Orlando
SACRIPANT'S man
TOM
RALPH
Fiddler
Several of the Twelve Peers of France, whose names are not given.
Clowns, Attendants, &c.
ANGELICA, daughter to Marsilius
MELISSA, an enchantress
Satyrs

THE HISTORY OF ORLANDO FURIOSO

Enter **MARSILIUS** and **ANGELICA**; the **SOLDAN, RODOMONT, MANDRICARD, BRANDIMART, ORLANDO,
SACRIPANT** and his **MAN**, with **OTHERS**.

MARSILIUS
Victorious princes, summon'd to appear
Within the continent of Africa;
From seven-fold Nilus to Taprobany,
Where fair Apollo darting forth his light
Plays on the seas;
From Gades' islands, where stout Hercules
Emblaz'd his trophies on two posts of brass,
To Tanais, whose swift-declining floods

Descended from the royal house of France,
And nephew to the mighty Charlemagne,
Surnam'd Orlando, the County Palatine.
Swift fame hath sounded to our western seas
The matchless beauty of Angelica,
Fairer than was the nymph of Mercury,
Who, when bright Phœbus mounteth up his coach,
And tracts Aurora in her silver steps,
And sprinkles from the folding of her lap
White lilies, roses, and sweet violets.
Yet thus believe me, princes of the south,
Although my country's love, dearer than pearl
Or mines of gold, might well have kept me back;
The sweet conversing with my king and friends,
Left all for love, might well have kept me back
The seas by Neptune hoisèd to the 'heavens,
Whose dangerous flaws might well have kept me back;
The savage Moors and Anthropophagi,
Whose lands I pass'd, might well have kept me back;
The doubt of entertainment in the court
When I arriv'd, might well have kept me back;
But so the fame of fair Angelica
Stamp'd in my thoughts the figure of her love,
As neither country, king, or seas, or cannibals,
Could by despairing keep Orlando back.
I list not boast in acts of chivalry,
(An humour never fitting with my mind,)
But come there forth the proudest champion
That hath suspicion in the Palatine,
And with thy trusty sword Durandell,
Single, I'll register upon his helm
What I dare do for fair Angelica.
But leaving these such glories as they be,
I love, my lord;
Angelica herself shall speak for me.

MARSILIUS
Daughter, thou hear'st what love hath here alleg'd,
How all these kings, by beauty summon'd here,
Put in their pleas, for hope of diadem,
Of noble deeds, of wealth, and chivalry,
All hoping to possess Angelica.
Sith father's will may hap to aim amiss,
(For parents' thoughts in love oft step awry,)
Choose thou the man who best contenteth thee,
And he shall wear the Afric crown next me.
For trust me, daughter, like of whom thou please,
Thou satisfied, my thoughts shall be at ease.

ANGELICA

Kings of the south, viceroys of Africa,
Sith father's will hangs on his daughter's choice,
And I, as erst Princess Andromache
Seated amidst the crew of Priam's sons,
Have liberty to choose where best I love;
Must freely say, for fancy hath no fraud,
That far unworthy is Angelica
Of such as deign to grace her with their loves;
The Soldan with his seat in Babylon,
The Prince of Cuba, and of Mexico.
Whose wealthy crowns might win a woman's will,
Young Brandimart, master of all the isles
Where Neptune planted hath his treasury;
The worst of these men of so high import
As may command a greater dame than I.
But fortune, or some deep-inspiring fate,
Venus, or else the bastard brat of Mars,
Whose bow commands the motions of the mind,
Hath sent proud love to enter such a plea
As nonsuits all your princely evidence,
And flat commands that, maugre majesty,
I choose Orlando, County Palatine.

RODOMONT

How likes Marsilius of his daughter's choice?

MARSILIUS

As fits Marsilius of his daughter's spouse.

RODOMONT

Highly thou wrong'st us, King of Africa,
To brave thy neighbour princes with disgrace,
To tie thine honour to thy daughter's thoughts,
Whose choice is like that Greekish giglot's love,
That left her lord, Prince Menelaus,
And with a swain made scape away to Troy.
What is Orlando but a straggling mate,
Banish'd for some offence by Charlemagne,
Skipp'd from his country as Anchises' son,
And means, as he did to the Carthage Queen,
To pay her ruth and ruin for her love?

ORLANDO

Injurious Cuba, ill it fits thy gree
To wrong a stranger with discourtesy.
Were't not the sacred presence of Angelica

Prevails with me, as Venus' smiles with Mars,
To set a supersedeas of my wrath,
Soon should I teach thee what it were to brave.

MANDRICARD
And, Frenchman, were't not' gainst the law of arms,
In place of parley for to draw a sword,
Untaught companion, I would learn you know
What duty 'longs to such a prince as he.

ORLANDO
Then as did Hector 'fore Achilles' tent,
Trotting his courser softly on the plains,
Proudly dar'd forth the stoutest youth of Greece;
So who stands highest in his own conceit,
And thinks his courage can perform the most,
Let him but throw his gauntlet on the ground,
And I will pawn my honour to his gage,
He shall ere night be met and combated.

MARSILIUS
Shame you not, princes, at this bad agree,
To wrong a stranger with discourtesy?
Believe me, lords, my daughter hath made choice,
And, maugre him that thinks him most aggriev'd,
She shall enjoy the County Palatine.

BRANDIMART
But would these princes follow my advice,
And enter arms as did the Greeks 'gainst Troy,
Nor he, nor thou shouldst have Angelica.

RODOMONT
Let him be thought a dastard to his death,
That will not sell the travails he hath past
Dearer than for a woman's fooleries:
What says the mighty Mandricard?

MANDRICARD
I vow to hie me home to Mexico,
To troop myself with such a crew of men
As shall so fill the downs of Africa,
Like to the plains of watery Thessaly,
Whenas an eastern gale whistling aloft
Hath overspread the ground with grasshoppers.
Then see, Marsilius, if the Palatine
Can keep his love from falling to our lots,
Or thou canst keep thy country free from spoil.

MARSILIUS
Why, think you, lords, with haughty menaces
To dare me out within my palace-gates?
Or hope you to make conquest by constraint
Of that which never could be got by love?
Pass from my court, make haste out of my land,
Stay not within the bounds Marsilius holds;
Lest, little brooking these unfitting braves,
My choler overslip the law of arms,
And I inflict revenge on such abuse.

RODOMONT
I'll beard and brave thee in thy proper town,
And here ensconce myself despite of thee,
And hold thee play till Mandricard return.—
What says the mighty Soldan of Egýpt?

SOLDAN
That when Prince Menelaus with all his mates
Had ten years held their siege in Asia,
Folding their wraths in cinders of fair Troy,
Yet, for their arms grew by conceit of love,
Their trophies were but conquest of a girl:
Then trust me, lords, I'll never manage arms
For women's loves that are so quickly lost.

BRANDIMART
Tush, my lords, why stand you upon terms?
Let 's to our sconce,—and you, my lord, to Mexico.

ORLANDO
Ay, sirs, ensconce ye how you can,
See what we dare, and thereon set your rest.

[Exeunt all except **SACRIPANT** and his **MAN**.

SACRIPANT [Aside]
Boast not too much, Marsilius, in thyself,
Nor of contentment in Angelica;
For Sacripant must have Angelica,
And with her Sacripant must have the crown:
By hook or crook I must and will have both.
Ah sweet Revenge, incense their angry minds,
Till, all these princes weltering in their bloods,
The crown do fall to County Sacripant!
Sweet are the thoughts that smother from conceit:
For when I come and set me down to rest,

My chair presents a throne of majesty;
And when I set my bonnet on my head,
Methinks I fit my forehead for a crown;
And when I take my truncheon in my fist,
A sceptre then comes tumbling in my thoughts;
My dreams are princely, all of diadems.
Honour,—methinks the title is too base:
Mighty, glorious, and excellent,—ay, these,
My glorious genius, sound within my mouth;
These please the ear, and with a sweet applause
Make me in terms coequal with the gods.
Then these, Sacripant, and none but these;
And these, or else make hazard of thy life.
Let it suffice, I will conceal the rest.—
Sirrah.

MAN
My lord?

SACRIPANT [Aside]
My lord! How basely was this slave brought up,
That knows no titles fit for dignity,
To grace his master with hyperboles!
My lord! why, the basest baron of fair Africa
Deserves as much: yet County Sacripant
Must he a swain salute with name of lord.—
Sirrah, what thinks the Emperor of my colours,
Because in field I wear both blue and red at once?

MAN
They deem, my lord, your honour lives at peace,
As one that's neuter in these mutinies,
And covets to rest equal friend to both;
Neither envious to Prince Mandricard,
Nor wishing ill unto Marsilius,
That you may safely pass where'er you please,
With friendly salutations from them both.

SACRIPANT
Ay, so they guess, but level far awry;
For if they knew the secrets of my thoughts,
Mine emblem sorteth to another sense.
I wear not these as one resolv'd to peace,
But blue and red as enemy to both;
Blue, as hating King Marsilius,
And red, as in revenge to Mandricard;
Foe unto both, friend only to myself,
And to the crown, for that's the golden mark

Which makes my thoughts dream on a diadem.
See'st not thou all men presage I shall be king?
Marsilius sends to me for peace; Mandricard
Puts off his cap, ten mile off: two things more,
And then I cannot miss the crown.

MAN
O, what be those, my good lord?

SACRIPANT
First must
I get the love of fair Angelica.
Now am I full of amorous conceits,
Not that I doubt to have what I desire,
But how I might best with mine honour woo:
Write, or entreat,—fie, that fitteth not;
Send by ambassadors,—no, that's too base;
Flatly command,—ay, that's for Sacripant:
Say thou art Sacripant, and art in love,
And who
In Africa dare say the county nay?
O Angelica,
Fairer than Chloris when in all her pride
Bright Maia's son entrapp'd her in the net
Wherewith Vulcan entangled the god of war!

MAN
Your honour is so far in contemplation of Angelica as you have forgot the second thing in attaining to the crown.

SACRIPANT
That's to be done by poison,
Prowess, or any means of treachery,
To put to death the traitorous Orlando.—
But who is this comes here? Stand close.

[They retire.

[Enter **ORGALIO**.

ORGALIO
I am sent on embassage to the right mighty and magnificent, alias, the right proud and pontifical, the County Sacripant; for Marsilius and Orlando, knowing him to be as full of prowess as policy, and fearing lest in leaning to the other faction he might greatly prejudice them, they seek first to hold the candle before the devil, and knowing him to be a Thrasonical mad-cap, they have sent me a Gnathonical companion, to give him lettuce fit for his lips. Now, sir, knowing his astronomical humours, as one that gazeth so high at the stars as he never looketh on the pavement in the streets—but, whist! lupus est in fabula.

SACRIPANT [Coming forward]
Sirrah, thou that ruminatest to thyself a catalogue of privy conspiracies, what art thou?

ORGALIO
God save your majesty!

SACRIPANT [Aside]
My majesty!—Come hither, my well-nutrimented knave: whom takest thou me to be?

ORGALIO
The mighty Mandricard of Mexico.

SACRIPANT [Aside]
I hold these salutations as ominous; for saluting me by that which I am not, he presageth what I shall be; for so did the Lacedæmonians by Agathocles, who of a base potter wore the kingly diadem.—But why deemest thou me to be the mighty Mandricard of Mexico?

ORGALIO
Marry, sir,—

SACRIPANT
Stay there: wert thou never in France?

ORGALIO
Yes, if it please your majesty.

SACRIPANT
So it seems, for there they salute their king by the name of Sir,
Monsieur:—but forward.

ORGALIO
Such sparks of peerless majesty
From those looks flame, like lightning from the east,
As either Mandricard, or else some greater prince,—

SACRIPANT [Aside]
Methinks these salutations make my thoughts
To be heroical.—
But say, to whom art thou sent?

ORGALIO
To the County Sacripant.

SACRIPANT
Why, I am he.

ORGALIO

It pleaseth your majesty to jest.

SACRIPANT
Whate'er I seem, I tell thee I am he.

ORGALIO
Then may it please your honour, the Emperor Marsilius, together with his daughter Angelica and Orlando, entreateth your excellency to dine with them.

SACRIPANT
Is Angelica there?

ORGALIO
There, my good lord.

SACRIPANT
Sirrah.

MAN
My lord?

SACRIPANT
Villain, Angelica sends for me: see that
Thou entertain that happy messenger,
And bring him in with thee.

[Exeunt.

[Enter **ORLANDO**, the **DUKE OF AQUITAIN**, and the **COUNTY ROSSILION**, with **SOLDIERS**.

ORLANDO
Princes of France, the sparkling light of fame,
Whose glory's brighter than the burnish'd gates
From whence Latona's lordly son doth march,
When, mounted on his coach tinsell'd with flames,
He triumphs in the beauty of the heavens;
This is the place where Rodomont lies hid:
Here lies he, like the thief of Thessaly,
Which scuds abroad and searcheth for his prey,
And, being gotten, straight he gallops home,
As one that dares not break a spear in field.
But trust me, princes, I have girt his fort,
And I will sack it, or on this castle-wall
I'll write my resolution with my blood:—
Therefore, drum, sound a parle.

[A parle is sounded, and a **SOLDIER** comes upon the walls.

SOLDIER
Who is that troubleth our sleeps?

ORLANDO
Why, sluggard, seest thou not Lycaon's son,
The hardy plough-swain unto mighty Jove,
Hath trac'd his silver furrows in the heavens.
And, turning home his over-watchèd team,
Gives leave unto Apollo's chariot?
I tell thee, sluggard, sleep is far unfit
For such as still have hammering in their heads
But only hope of honour and revenge:
These call'd me forth to rouse thy master up.
Tell him from me, false coward as he is,
That Orlando, the County Palatine,
Is come this morning, with a band of French,
To play him hunt's-up with a point of war:
I'll be his minstrel with my drum and fife;
Bid him come forth, and dance it if he dare,
Let fortune throw her favours where she list.

SOLDIER
Frenchman, between half-sleeping and awake,
Although the misty veil strain'd over Cynthia
Hinders my sight from noting all thy crew,
Yet, for I know thee and thy straggling grooms
Can in conceit build castles in the sky,
But in your actions like the stammering Greek
Which breathes his courage bootless in the air,
I wish thee well, Orlando, get thee gone,
Say that a sentinel did suffer thee;
For if the round or court-of-guard should hear
Thou or thy men were braying at the walls,
Charles' wealth, the wealth of all his western mines,
Found in the mountains of Transalpine France,
Might not pay ransom to the king for thee.

ORLANDO
Brave sentinel, if nature hath enchas'd
A sympathy of courage to thy tale,
And, like the champion of Andromache,
Thou, or thy master, dare come out the gates,
Maugre the watch, the round, or court-of-guard,
I will attend to abide the coward here.
If not, but still the craven sleeps secure,
Pitching his guard within a trench of stones,
Tell him his walls shall serve him for no proof,
But as the son of Saturn in his wrath

Pash'd all the mountains at Typhœus' head,
And topsy-turvy turn'd the bottom up,—
So shall the castle of proud Rodomont.—
And so, brave lords of France, let's to the fight.

[Exeunt.

[Alarums: **RODOMONT** and **BRANDIMART** fly.

[Enter **ORLANDO** with Rodomont's coat.

ORLANDO
The fox is scap'd, but here's his case:
I miss'd him near; 'twas time for him to trudge.

[Enter the **DUKE OF AQUITAIN**.

How now, my lord of Aquitain!

DUKE OF AQUITAIN
My lord,
The court-of-guard is put unto the sword,
And all the watch that thought themselves so sure,
So that not one within the castle breathes.

ORLANDO
Come, then,
Let's post amain to find out Rodomont,
And then in triumph march unto Marsilius.

[Exeunt.

[Enter **MEDOR** and **ANGELICA**.

ANGELICA
I marvel, Medor, what my father means
To enter league with County Sacripant?

MEDOR
Madam, the king your father's wise enough;
He knows the county, like to Cassius,
Sits sadly dumping, aiming Cæsar's death,
Yet crying "Ave" to his majesty.
But, madam, mark a while, and you shall see
Your father shake him off from secrecy.

ANGELICA
So much I guess; for when he will'd I should

Give entertainment to the doting earl,
His speech was ended with a frowning smile.

MEDOR
Madam, see where he comes: I will be gone.

[Exit.

[Enter **SACRIPANT** and his **MAN**.

SACRIPANT
How fares my fair Angelica?

ANGELICA
Well, that my lord so friendly is in league,
As honour wills him, with Marsilius.

SACRIPANT
Angelica, shall I have a word or two with thee?

ANGELICA
What pleaseth my lord for to command.

SACRIPANT
Then know, my love, I cannot paint my grief,
Nor tell a tale of Venus and her son,
Reporting such a catalogue of toys:
It fits not Sacripant to be effeminate.
Only give leave, my fair Angelica,
To say, the county is in love with thee.

ANGELICA
Pardon, my lord; my loves are over-past:
So firmly is Orlando printed in my thoughts,
As love hath left no place for any else.

SACRIPANT
Why, over-weening damsel, see'st thou not
Thy lawless love unto this straggling mate
Hath fill'd our Afric regions full of blood?
And wilt thou still perséver in thy love?
Tush, leave the Palatine, and go with me.

ANGELICA
Brave county, know, where sacred love unites,
The knot of gordian at the shrine of Jove
Was never half so hard or intricate
As be the bands which lovely Venus ties.

Sweet is my love; and, for I love, my lord,
Seek not unless, as Alexander did,
To cut the plough-swain's traces with thy sword,
Or slice the slender fillets of my life:
Or else, my lord, Orlando must be mine.

SACRIPANT
Stand I on love? stoop I to Venus' lure,
That never yet did fear the god of war?
Shall men report that County Sacripant
Held lovers' pains for pining passions?
Shall such a siren offer me more wrong
Than they did to the prince of Ithaca?
No;
As he his ears, so, county, stop thine eye.
Go to your needle, lady, and your clouts;
Go to such milksops as are fit for love:
I will employ my busy brains for war.

ANGELICA
Let not, my lord, denial breed offence:
Love doth allow her favours but to one,
Nor can there sit within the sacred shrine
Of Venus more than one installèd heart.
Orlando is the gentleman I love,
And more than he may not enjoy my love.

SACRIPANT
Damsel, be gone: fancy hath taken leave;
Where I took hurt, there have I heal'd myself,
As those that with Achilles' lance were wounded,
Fetch'd help at self-same pointed spear.
Beauty gan brave, and beauty hath repulse;
And, beauty, get ye gone to your Orlando.

[Exit **ANGELICA**.

MAN
My lord, hath love amated him whose thoughts
Have ever been heroical and brave?
Stand you in dumps, like to the Myrmidon
Trapt in the tresses of Polyxena,
Who, mid the glory of his chivalry,
Sat daunted with a maid of Asia?

SACRIPANT
Think'st thou my thoughts are lunacies of love?
No, they are brands firèd in Pluto's forge,

Where sits Tisiphone tempering in flames
Those torches that do set on fire revenge.
I lov'd the dame; but brav'd by her repulse,
Hate calls me on to quittance all my ills;
Which first must come by offering prejudice
Unto Orlando her belovèd love.

MAN
O, how may that be brought to pass, my lord?

SACRIPANT
Thus.
Thou see'st that Medor and Angelica
Are still so secret in their private walks,
As that they trace the shady lawnds,
And thickest-shadow'd groves,
Which well may breed suspicion of some love.
Now, than the French no nation under heaven
Is sooner touch'd with stings of jealousy.

MAN
And what of that, my lord?

SACRIPANT
Hard by, for solace, in a secret grove,
The county once a-day fails not to walk:
There solemnly he ruminates his love.
Upon those shrubs that compass-in the spring,
And on those trees that border-in those walks,
I'll slily have engraven on every bark
The names of Medor and Angelica.
Hard by, I'll have some roundelays hung up,
Wherein shall be some posies of their loves,
Fraughted so full of fiery passions
As that the county shall perceive by proof
Medor hath won his fair Angelica.

MAN
Is this all, my lord?

SACRIPANT
No;
For thou like to a shepherd shalt be cloth'd,
With staff and bottle, like some country-swain
That tends his flocks feeding upon these downs.
There see thou buzz into the county's ears
That thou hast often seen within these woods
Base Medor sporting with Angelica;

And when he hears a shepherd's simple tale,
He will not think 'tis feign'd.
Then either a madding mood will end his love,
Or worse betide him through fond jealousy.

MAN
Excellent, my lord: see how I will play the shepherd.

SACRIPANT
And mark thou how I will play the carver:
Therefore be gone, and make thee ready straight.

[Exit his **MAN**: **SACRIPANT** carves the names and, hangs up the roundelays on the trees, and then goes out; and his **MAN** re-enters like a shepherd.

MAN
Thus all alone, and like a shepherd's swain,
As Paris, when Œnone lov'd him well,
Forgat he was the son of Priamus,
All clad in grey, sat piping on a reed;
So I transformèd to this country shape,
Haunting these groves to work my master's will,
To plague the Palatine with jealousy,
And to conceit him with some deep extreme.—
Here comes the man unto his wonted walk.

[Enter **ORLANDO** and **ORGALIO**.

ORLANDO
Orgalio, go see a sentinel be plac'd,
And bid the soldiers keep a court-of-guard,
So to hold watch till secret here alone
I meditate upon the thoughts of love.

ORGALIO
I will, my lord.

[Exit.

ORLANDO
Fair queen of love, thou mistress of delight,
Thou gladsome lamp that wait'st on Phœbe's train,
Spreading thy kindness through the jarring orbs,
That in their union praise thy lasting powers;
Thou that hast stay'd the fiery Phlegon's course,
And mad'st the coachman of the glorious wain
To droop, in view of Daphne's excellence;
Fair pride of morn, sweet beauty of the even.

Look on Orlando languishing in love.
Sweet solitary groves, whereas the Nymphs
With pleasance laugh to see the Satyrs play,
Witness Orlando's faith unto his love.
Tread she these lawnds, kind Flora, boast thy pride.
Seek she for shade, spread, cedars, for her sake.
Fair Flora, make her couch amidst thy flowers.
Sweet crystal springs,
Wash ye with roses when she longs to drink.
Ah, thought, my heaven! ah, heaven, that knows my thought!
Smile, joy in her that my content hath wrought.

MAN [Aside]
The heaven of love is but a pleasant hell,
Where none but foolish-wise imprison'd dwell.

ORLANDO
Orlando, what contrarious thoughts be these,
That flock with doubtful motions in thy mind?
Heaven smiles, and trees do boast their summer pride.
What! Venus writes her triumphs here beside.

MAN [Aside]
Yet when thine eye hath seen, thy heart shall rue
The tragic chance that shortly shall ensue.

ORLANDO [Reads]
"Angelica:"—ah, sweet and heavenly name,
Life to my life, and essence to my joy!
But, soft!
This gordian knot together co-unites
A Medor partner in her peerless love.
Unkind, and will she bend her thoughts to change?
Her name, her writing! Foolish and unkind!
No name of hers, unless the brooks relent
To hear her name, and Rhodanus vouchsafe
To raise his moisten'd locks from out the reeds,
And flow with calm alongst his turning bounds:
No name of hers, unless the Zephyr blow
Her dignities alongst Ardenia woods,
Where all the world for wonders do await.
And yet her name! for why Angelica;
But, mix'd with Medor, not Angelica.
Only by me was lov'd Angelica,
Only for me must live Angelica.
I find her drift: perhaps the modest pledge
Of my content hath with a secret smile
And sweet disguise restrain'd her fancy thus,

Figuring Orlando under Medor's name;
Fine drift, fair nymph! Orlando hopes no less.

[Spies the roundelays.

Yet more! are Muses masking in these trees,
Framing their ditties in conceited lines,
Making a goddess, in despite of me,
That have no other but Angelica?

MAN [Aside]
Poor hapless man, these thoughts contain thy hell!

ORLANDO [Reads]
"Angelica is lady of his heart,
Angelica is substance of his joy,
Angelica is medicine of his smart,
Angelica hath healèd his annoy."
[Looks up]
Ah, false Angelica!—What, have we more?
[Reads]
"Let groves, let rocks, let woods, let watery springs,
The cedar, cypress, laurel, and the pine,
Joy in the notes of love that Medor sings
Of those sweet looks, Angelica, of thine.
Then, Medor, in Angelica take delight,
Early, at morn, at noon, at even, and night."
[Looks up]
What, dares Medor court my Venus?
What may Orlando deem?
Ætna, forsake the bounds of Sicily,
For now in me thy restless flames appear.
Refus'd, contemn'd, disdain'd! what worse than these?—
Orgalio!

[Re-enter **ORGALIO**.

ORGALIO
My lord?

ORLANDO
Boy, view these trees carvèd with true-love knots,
The inscription "Medor and Angelica;"
And read these verses hung up of their loves:
Now tell me, boy, what dost thou think?

ORGALIO
By my troth, my lord, I think Angelica is a woman.

ORLANDO
And what of that?

ORGALIO
Therefore unconstant, mutable, having their loves hanging in their eyelids; that as they are got with a look, so they are lost again with a wink. But here's a shepherd; it may be he can tell us news.

ORLANDO
What messenger hath Ate sent abroad
With idle looks to listen my laments?—
Sirrah, who wrongèd happy nature so,
To spoil these trees with this Angelica?—
Yet in her name, Orlando, they are blest.

MAN
I am a shepherd-swain, thou wandering knight,
That watch my flocks, not one that follow love.

ORLANDO
As follow love! dar'st thou dispraise my heaven,
Or once disgrace or prejudice her name?
Is not Angelica the queen of love,
Deck'd with the compound wreath of Adon's flowers?
She is. Then speak, thou peasant, what is he
That dares attempt to court my queen of love,
Or I shall send thy soul to Charon's charge.

MAN
Brave knight, since fear of death enforceth still
In greater minds submission and relent,
Know that this Medor, whose unhappy name
Is mixèd with the fair Angelica's,
Is even that Medor that enjoys her love.
Yon cave bears witness of their kind content;
Yon meadows talk the actions of their joy;
Our shepherds in their songs of solace sing,
"Angelica doth none but Medor love."

ORLANDO
Angelica doth none but Medor love!
Shall Medor, then, possess Orlando's love?
Dainty and gladsome beams of my delight,
Delicious brows, why smile your heavens for those
That, wounding you, prove poor Orlando's foes?
Lend me your plaints, you sweet Arcadian nymphs,
That wont to sing your new-departed loves;
Thou weeping flood, leave Orpheus' wail for me;

And, Titan's nieces, gather all in one
Those fluent springs of your lamenting tears,
And let them stream along my faintfull looks.

MAN [Aside]
Now is the fire, late smother'd in suspect,
Kindled, and burns within his angry breast:
Now have I done the will of Sacripant.

ORLANDO
Fœmineum servile genus, crudele, superbum:
Discourteous women, nature's fairest ill,
The woe of man, that first-created curse,
Base female sex, sprung from black Ate's loins,
Proud, disdainful, cruel, and unjust,
Whose words are shaded with enchanting wiles,
Worse than Medusa mateth all our minds;
And in their hearts sits shameless treachery,
Turning a truthless vile circumference.
O, could my fury paint their furies forth!
For hell's no hell, comparèd to their hearts,
Too simple devils to conceal their arts;
Born to be plagues unto the thoughts of men,
Brought for eternal pestilence to the world.
O femminile ingegno, de tutti mali sede,
Come ti volgi e muti facilmente,
Contrario oggetto proprio de la fede!
O infelice, o miser chi ti crede!
Importune, superbe, dispettose,
Prive d'amor, di fede, e di consiglio,
Temerarie, crudeli, inique, ingrate,
Per pestilenzia eterna al mondo nate.—
Villain, what art thou that followest me?

ORGALIO
Alas, my lord, I am your servant, Orgalio.

ORLANDO
No, villain, thou art Medor;
That rann'st away with Angelica.

ORGALIO
No, by my troth, my lord, I am Orgalio;
Ask all these people else.

ORLANDO
Art thou Orgalio? tell me where Medor is.

ORGALIO
My lord, look where he sits.

ORLANDO
What, sits he here, and braves me too?

MAN
No, truly, sir, I am not he.

ORLANDO
Yes, villain.

[Draws him in by the leg.

ORGALIO
Help, help, my Lord of Aquitain!

[Enter the **DUKE OF AQUITAIN** and **SOLDIERS**.

O, my Lord of Aquitain, the Count Orlando is run mad, and taking of a shepherd by the heels, rends him as one would tear a lark! See where he comes, with a leg on his neck.

[Re-enter **ORLANDO** with a leg.

ORLANDO
Villain, provide me straight a lion's skin,
Thou see'st I now am mighty Hercules;
Look where's my massy club upon my neck.
I must to hell,
To seek for Medor and Angelica,
Or else I die.
You that are the rest, get you quickly away;
Provide ye horses all of burnish'd gold,
Saddles of cork, because I'll have them light;
For Charlemagne the great is up in arms,
And Arthur with a crew of Britons comes
To seek for Medor and Angelica

[So he beateth them all in before him, except **ORGALIO**.

[Enter **MARSILIUS**.

ORGALIO
Ah, my lord, Orlando—

MARSILIUS
Orlando! what of Orlando?

ORGALIO

He, my lord, runs madding through the woods,
Like mad Orestes in his greatest rage.
Step but aside into the bordering grove,
There shall you see engraven on every tree
The lawless love of Medor and Angelica.
O, see, my lord, not any shrub but bears
The cursèd stamp that wrought the county's rage.
If thou be'st mighty King Marsilius,
For whom the county would adventure life,
Revenge it on the false Angelica.

MARSILIUS

Trust me, Orgalio, Theseus in his rage
Did never more revenge his wrong'd Hippolytus
Than I will on the false Angelica.
Go to my court, and drag me Medor forth;
Tear from his breast the daring villain's heart.
Next take that base and damn'd adulteress,—
I scorn to title her with daughter's name,—
Put her in rags, and, like some shepherdess,
Exile her from my kingdom presently.
Delay not, good Orgalio, see it done.

[Exit **ORGALIO**.

[Enter a **SOLDIER**, with **MANDRICARD** disguised.

How now, my friend! what fellow hast thou there?

SOLDIER

He says, my lord,
That he is servant unto Mandricard.

MARSILIUS

To Mandricard!
It fits me not to sway the diadem,
Or rule the wealthy realms of Barbary,
To stain my thoughts with any cowardice.—
Thy master brav'd me to my teeth,
He back'd the Prince of Cuba for my foe;
For which nor he nor his shall scape my hands.
No, soldier, think me resolute as he.

MANDRICARD

It grieves me much that princes disagree,
Sith black repentance followeth afterward:
But leaving that, pardon me, gracious lord.

MARSILIUS

For thou entreat'st, and newly art arriv'd,
And yet thy sword is not imbru'd in blood,
Upon conditions, I will pardon thee,—
That thou shalt never tell thy master, Mandricard,
Nor any fellow-soldier of the camp,
That King Marsilius licens'd thee depart:
He shall not think I am so much his friend,
That he or one of his shall scape my hand.

MANDRICARD

I swear, my lord, and vow to keep my word.

MARSILIUS

Then take my banderol of red;
Mine, and none but mine, shall honour thee,
And safe conduct thee to Port Carthagene.

MANDRICARD

But say, my lord, if Mandricard were here,
What favour should he find, or life or death?

MARSILIUS

I tell thee, friend, it fits not for a king
To prize his wrath before his courtesy.
Were Mandricard, the King of Mexico,
In prison here, and crav'd but liberty,
So little hate hangs in Marsilius' breast,
As one entreaty should quite raze it out.
But this concerns not thee, therefore, farewell.

MANDRICARD

Thanks, and good fortune fall to such a king
As covets to be counted courteous.

[Exit **MARSILIUS**.

Blush, Mandricard;
The honour of thy foe disgraceth thee;
Thou wrongest him that wisheth thee but well;
Thou bringest store of men from Mexico
To battle him that scorns to injure thee,
Pawning his colours for thy warrantize.
Back to thy ships, and hie thee to thy home;
Budge not a foot to aid Prince Rodomont;
But friendly gratulate these favours found,
And meditate on naught but to be friends.

[Exeunt.

[Enter **ORLANDO** attired like a madman.

ORLANDO
Woods, trees, leaves; leaves, trees, woods; tria sequuntur tria.—Ho, Minerva! salve, good morrow; how do you to-day? Tell me, sweet goddess, will Jove send Mercury to Calypso, to let me go? will he? why, then, he's a gentleman, every hair o' the head on him.—But, ho, Orgalio! where art thou, boy?

[Enter **ORGALIO**.

ORGALIO
Here, my lord: did you call me?

ORGALIO
No, nor name thee.

ORGALIO
Then God be with you.

[Proffers to go in.

ORLANDO
Nay, prithee, good Orgalio, stay: canst thou not tell me what to say?

ORGALIO
No, by my troth.

ORLANDO
O, this it is; Angelica is dead.

ORGALIO
Why, then, she shall be buried.

ORLANDO
But my Angelica is dead.

ORGALIO
Why, it may be so.

ORLANDO
But she's dead and buried.

ORGALIO
Ay, I think so.

ORLANDO
Nothing but "I think so," and "It may be so"!

[Beats him.

ORGALIO
What do you mean, my lord?

ORLANDO
Why, shall I tell you that my love is dead,
And can ye not weep for her?

ORGALIO
Yes, yes, my lord, I will.

ORLANDO
Well, do so, then. Orgalio.

ORGALIO
My lord?

ORLANDO
Angelica is dead.

[**ORGALIO** cries.

Ah, poor slave! so, cry no more now.

ORGALIO
Nay, I have quickly done.

ORLANDO
Orgalio.

ORGALIO
My lord?

ORLANDO
Medor's Angelica is dead.

[**ORGALIO** cries, and **ORLANDO** beats him again.

ORGALIO
Why do you beat me, my lord?

ORLANDO
Why, slave, wilt thou weep for Medor's Angelica? thou must laugh for her.

ORGALIO
Laugh! yes, I'll laugh all day, an you will.

ORLANDO
Orgalio.

ORGALIO
My lord?

ORLANDO
Medor's Angelica is dead.

ORGALIO
Ha, ha, ha, ha!

ORLANDO
So, 'tis well now.

ORGALIO
Nay, this is easier than the other was.

ORLANDO
Now away!
Seek the herb moly; for I must to hell,
To seek for Medor and Angelica.

ORGALIO
I know not the herb moly, i' faith.

ORLANDO
Come, I'll lead ye to it by the ears.

ORGALIO
'Tis here, my lord, 'tis here.

ORLANDO
'Tis indeed.
Now to Charon, bid him dress his boat,
For he had never such a passenger.

ORGALIO
Shall I tell him your name?

ORLANDO
No, then he will be afraid, and not be at home.

[Exit **ORGALIO**.

[Enter **TOM** and **RALPH**.

TOM
Sirrah Ralph, and thou'lt go with me, I'll let thee see the bravest madman that ever thou sawest.

RALPH
Sirrah Tom, I believe it was he that was at our town o' Sunday: I'll tell thee what he did, sirrah. He came to our house, when all our folks were gone to church, and there was nobody at home but I, and I was turning of the spit, and he comes in, and bade me fetch him some drink. Now, I went and fetched him some; and ere I came again, by my troth, he ran away with the roast meat, spit and all, and so we had nothing but porridge to dinner.

TOM
By my troth, that was brave: but, sirrah, he did so course the boys, last Sunday; and if ye call him madman, he'll run after you, and tickle your ribs so with his flap of leather that he hath, as it passeth.

[They spy **ORLANDO**.

RALPH
O, Tom, look where he is! call him madman.

TOM
Madman, madman.

RALPH
Madman, madman.

ORLANDO
What say'st thou, villian?

[Beats them.

So, now you shall be both my soliders.

TOM
Your soldiers! we shall have a mad captain, then.

ORLANDO
You must fight against Medor.

RALPH
Yes, let me alone with him for a bloody nose.

ORLANDO
Come, then, and I will give you weapons straight.

[Exeunt

[Enter **ANGELICA**, like a poor woman.

ANGELICA
Thus causeless banish'd from thy native home,
Here sit, Angelica, and rest a while,
For to bewail the fortunes of thy love.

[Enter **RODOMONT** and **BRANDIMART**, with **SOLDIERS**.

RODOMONT
This way she went, and far she cannot be.

BRANDIMART
See where she is, my lord: speak as if
You knew her not.

RODOMONT
Fair shepherdess, for so thy sitting seems,
Or nymph, for less thy beauty cannot be,
What, feed you sheep upon these downs?

ANGELICA
Daughter I am unto a bordering swain,
That tend my flocks within these shady groves.

RODOMONT
Fond girl, thou liest; thou art Angelica.

BRANDIMART
Ay, thou art she that wrong'd the Palatine.

ANGELICA
For I am known, albeit I am disguis'd,
Yet dare I turn the lie into thy throat,
Sith thou report'st I wrong'd the Palatine.

BRANDIMART
Nay, then, thou shalt be us'd according?
To thy deserts.—Come, bring her to our tents.

RODOMONT
But stay, what drum is this?

[Enter **ORLANDO** with a drum; **ORGALIO**; and **TOM**, **RALPH**, and other **CLOWNS**, as **SOLDIERS**, with spits
and dripping-pans.

BRANDIMART
Now see,

Angelica, the fruits of all your love.

ORLANDO
Soldiers,
This is the city of great Babylon,
Where proud Darius was rebated from:
Play but the men, and I will lay my head,
We'll sack and raze it ere the sun be set.

TOM
Yea, and scratch it too.—March fair, fellow frying-pan.

ORLANDO
Orgalio, knowest thou the cause of my laughter?

ORGALIO
No, by my troth, nor no wise man else.

ORLANDO
Why, sirrah, to think that if the enemy were fled ere we come, we'll not leave one of our own soldiers alive, for we two will kill them with our fists.

RALPH
Foh, come, let's go home again: he'll set probatum est upon my head-piece anon.

ORLANDO
No, no, thou shalt not be hurt,—nor thee.
Back, soldiers; look where the enemy is.

TOM
Captain, they have a woman amongst them.

ORLANDO
And what of that?

TOM
Why, strike you down the men, and then let me alone to thrust in the woman.

ORLANDO
No, I am challengèd the single fight.—
Sirrah, is't you challenge me the combat?

BRANDIMART
Frantic companion, lunatic and wood,
Get thee hence, or else I vow by heaven,
Thy madness shall not privilege thy life.

ORLANDO

I tell thee, villain, Medor wrong'd me so,
Sith thou art come his champion to the field,
I'll learn thee know I am the Palatine.

[Alarum: they fight; **ORLANDO** kills **BRANDIMART**; and all the rest fly, except **ANGELICA** and **ORGALIO**.

ORGALIO
Look, my lord, here's one killed.

ORLANDO
Who killed him?

ORGALIO
You, my lord, I think.

ORLANDO
I! no, no, I see who killed him.

[Goes to **ANGELICA**, and knows her not.

Come hither, gentle sir, whose prowess hath performed such an act: think not the courteous Palatine will hinder that thine honour hath achieved.—Orgalio, fetch me a sword, that presently this squire may be dubbed a knight.

ANGELICA [Aside]
Thanks, gentle fortune, that sends me such good hap,
Rather to die by him I love so dear,
Than live and see my lord thus lunatic.

ORGALIO [Giving a sword]
Here, my lord.

ORLANDO
If thou be'st come of Lancelot's worthy line,
Welcome thou art.
Kneel down, sir knight; rise up, sir knight;
Here, take this sword, and hie thee to the fight.

[Exit **ANGELICA** with the sword.

Now tell me, Orgalio, whatdost thou think?
will not this knight prove a valiant squire?

ORGALIO
He cannot choose, being of your making.

ORLANDO
But where's Angelica now?

ORGALIO
Faith, I cannot tell.

ORLANDO
Villain, find her out,
Or else the torments that Ixion feels,
The rolling stone, the tubs of the Belides—
Villain, wilt thou not find her out?

ORGALIO
Alas, my lord, I know not where she is.

ORLANDO
Run to Charlemagne, spare for no cost;
Tell him, Orlando sent for Angelica.

ORGALIO
Faith, I'll fetch you such an Angelica as you never saw before.

[Exit.

ORLANDO
As though that Sagittarius in his pride
Could take brave Leda from stout Jupiter!
And yet, forsooth, Medor, base Medor durst
Attempt to reave Orlando of his love.
Sirrah, you that are the messenger of Jove,
You that can sweep it through the milk-white path
That leads unto the senate-house of Mars,
Fetch me my shield temper'd of purest steel,
My helm
Forg'd by the Cyclops for Anchises' son,
And see if I dare combat for Angelica.

[Re-enter **ORGALIO**, with **TOM** dressed like Angelica.

ORGALIO
Come away, and take heed you laugh not.

TOM
No, I warrant you; but I think I had best go back and shave my beard.

ORGALIO
Tush, that will not be seen.

TOM
Well, you will give me the half-crown ye promised me?

ORGALIO
Doubt not of that, man.

TOM
Sirrah, didst not see me serve the fellow a fine trick, when we came over the market-place?

ORGALIO
Why, how was that?.

TOM
Why, he comes to me and said, "Gentlewoman, wilt please you take a pint or a quart?" "No gentlewoman," said I, "but your friend and Dority."

ORGALIO
Excellent!—Come, see where my lord is.
—My lord, here is Angelica.

ORLANDO
Mass, thou say'st true, 'tis she indeed.—How fares.
The fair Angelica?

TOM
Well, I thank you heartily.

ORLANDO
Why, art thou not that same Angelica,
With brows as bright as fair Erythea
That darks Canopus with her silver hue?

TOM
Yes, forsooth.

ORLANDO
Are not these the beauteous cheeks
Wherein the lilies and the native rose
Sit equal-suited with a blushing red?

TOM
He makes a garden-plot in my face.

ORLANDO
Are not, my dear, those the radiant eyes
Whereout proud Phœbus flasheth out his beams?

TOM
Yes, yes, with squibs and crackers bravely.

ORLANDO
You are Angelica?

TOM
Yes, marry, am I.

ORLANDO
Where's your sweetheart Medor?

TOM
Orgalio, give me eighteen-pence, and let me go.

ORLANDO
Speak, strumpet, speak.

TOM
Marry, sir, he is drinking a pint or a quart.

ORLANDO
Why, strumpet, worse than Mars his trothless love,
Falser than faithless Cressida! strumpet, 'thou shalt not scape.

TOM
Come, come, you do not use me like a gentlewomen: an if I be not for you, I am for another.

ORLANDO
Are you? that will I try.

[Beats him out, and exit, followed by **ORGALIO**.

[Enter the **TWELVE PEERS** of France, with drum and trumpets.

OGIER
Brave peers of France, sith we have pass'd the bounds,
Whereby the wrangling billows seek for straits
To war with Tellus and her fruitful mines;
Sith we have furrow'd through those wandering tides
Of Tyrrhene seas, and made our galleys dance
Upon the Hyperborean billows' crests,
That brave with streams the watery occident;
And found the rich and wealthy Indian clime
Sought-to by greedy minds for hurtful gold;
Now let us seek to venge the lamp of France
That lately was eclipsèd in Angelica;
Now let us seek Orlando forth, our peer,
Though from his former wits lately estrang'd,
Yet famous in our favours as before;
And, sith by chance weall encounter'd be,

Let's seek revenge on her that wrought his wrong.

NAMUS
But being thus arriv'd in place unknown,
Who shall direct our course unto the court
Where brave Marsilius keeps his royal state?

OGIER
Lo, here, two Indian palmers hard at hand,
Who can perhaps resolve our hidden doubts.

[Enter **MARSILIUS** and **MANDRICARD** like Palmers.

Palmers, God speed.

MARSILIUS
Lordings, we greet you well.

OGIER
Where lies Marsilius' court, friend, canst thou tell?

MARSILIUS
His court's his camp, the prince is now in arms.

TURPIN
In arms!
What's he that dares annoy so great a king?

MANDRICARD
Such as both love and fury do confound:
Fierce Sacripant, incens'd with strange desires,
Wars on Marsilius, and, Rodomont being dead,
Hath levied all his men, and traitor-like
Assails his lord and loving sovereign:
And Mandricard, who late hath been in arms
To prosecute revenge against Marsilius,
Is now through favours past become his friend.
Thus stands the state of matchless India.

OGIER
Palmer, I like thy brave and brief discourse;
And, couldst thou bring us to the prince's camp,
We would acknowledge friendship at thy hands

MARSILIUS
Ye stranger lords, why seek ye out Marsilius?

OLIVER

In hope that he, whose empire is so large,
Will make both mind and monarchy agree.

MARSILIUS
Whence are you, lords, and what request you here?

NAMUS
A question over-haughty for thy weed,
Fit for the king himself for to propound.

MANDRICARD
O, sir, know that under simple weeds
The gods have mask'd: then deem not with disdain
To answer to this palmer's question,
Whose coat includes perhaps as great as yours.

OGIER
Haughty their words, their persons full of state;
Though habit be but mean, their minds excell.—
Well, palmers, know
That princes are in India arriv'd,
Yea, even those western princely peers of France
That through the world adventures undertake,
To find Orlando late incens'd with rage.
Then, palmers, sith you know our styles and state,
Advise us where your king Marsilius is.

MARSILIUS
Lordings of France, here is Marsilius,
That bids you welcome into India,
And will in person bring you to his camp.

OGIER
Marsilius! and thus disguis'd!

MARSILIUS
Even Marsilius and thus disguis'd.
But what request these princes at my hand?

TURPIN
We sue for lawand justice at thy hand:
We seek Angelica thy daughter out,
That wanton maid, that hath eclips'd the joy
Of royal France, and made Orlando mad.

MARSILIUS
My daughter, lords! why, she is exil'd;
And her griev'd father is content to lose

The pleasance of his age, to countenance law.

OLIVER
Not only exile shall await Angelica,
But death and bitter death shall follow her.
Then yield us right, Marsilius, or our swords
Shall make thee fear to wrong the peers of France.

MARSILIUS
Words cannot daunt me, princes, be assur'd;
But law and justice shall o'er-rule in this,
And I will bury father's name and love.
The hapless maid, banish'd from out my land,
Wanders about in woods and ways unknown:
Her, if ye find, with fury persecute;
I now disdain the name to be her father.
Lords of France, what would you more of me?

OGIER
Marsilius, we commend thy princely mind,
And will report thy justice through the world.—
Come, peers of France, let's seek Angelica,
Left for a spoil to our revenging thoughts.

[Exeunt.

[Enter **ORLANDO** like a poet, and **ORGALIO**.

ORLANDO
Orgalio,
Is not my love like those purple-colour'd swans
That gallop by the coach of Cynthia?

ORGALIO
Yes, marry, is she, my lord.

ORLANDO
Is not her face silver'd like that milk-white shape
That Jove came dancing in to Semele?

ORGALIO
It is, my lord.

ORLANDO
Then go thy ways, and climb up to the clouds,
And tell Apollo that Orlando sits
Making of verses for Angelica.
If he deny to send me down the shirt

Which Deianira sent to Hercules,
To make me brave upon my wedding-day,
Tell him
I'll pass the Alps, and up to Meroe,
(I know he knows that watery lakish hill,)
And pull the harp out of the minstrel's hands,
And pawn it unto lovely Proserpine,
That she may fetch the fair Angelica.

ORGALIO
But, my lord, Apollo is asleep, and will not hear me.

ORLANDO
Then tell him, he is a sleepy knave: but, sirrah, let nobody trouble me, for I must lie down a while, and talk with the stars.

[Lies down and sleeps.

[Enter a **FIDDLER**.

ORGALIO
What, old acquaintance! well met.

FIDDLER
Ho, you would have me play Angelica again, would ye not?

ORGALIO
No, but I can tell thee where thou mayst earn two or three shillings this morning, even with the turning of a hand.

FIDDLER
Two or three shillings! tush, thou wot cozen me, thou: but an thou canst tell where I may earn a groat, I'll give thee sixpence for thy pains.

ORGALIO
Then play a fit of mirth to my lord.

FIDDLER
Why, he is mad still, is he not?

ORGALIO
No, no: come, play.

FIDDLER
At which side doth he use to give his reward?

ORGALIO
Why, of any side.

FIDDLER
Doth he not use to throw the chamberpot sometimes? 'Twould grieve me he should wet my fiddle-strings.

ORGALIO
Tush, I warrant thee.

[**FIDDLER** plays and sings any odd toy, and **ORLANDO** wakes.

ORLANDO
Who is this? Shan Cuttelero! Heartily welcome, Shan Cuttelero.

FIDDLER
No, sir, you should have said "Shan the Fidideldero."

ORLANDO
What, hast thou brought me my sword?

[Takes away his fiddle.

FIDDLER
A sword! no, no, sir, that's my fiddle.

ORLANDO
But dost thou think the temper to be good?
And will it hold
When thus and thus we Medor do assail?

[Strikes and beats him with the fiddle.

FIDDLER
Lord, sir, you'll break my living!—You told me your master was not mad.

ORLANDO
Tell me, why hast thou marr'd my sword?
The pummel's well, the blade is curtal short:
Villain, why hast thou made it so?

[Breaks the fiddle about his head.

FIDDLER
O Lord, sir, will you answer this?

[Exit.

[Enter **MELISSA** with a glass of wine.

ORLANDO

Orgalio, who is this?

ORGALIO

Faith, my lord, some old witch, I think.

MELISSA

O, that my lord would but conceit my tale!
Then would I speak and hope to find redress.

ORLANDO

Fair Polyxena, the pride of Ilion,
Fear not Achilles' over-madding boy;
Pyrrhus shall not, &c.—
Souns, Orgalio, why sufferest thou this old trot to come so nigh me?

ORGALIO

Come, come, stand by, your breath stinks.

ORLANDO

What! be all the Trojans fied?
Then give me some drink.

MELISSA

Here, Palatine, drink;
And ever be thou better for this draught.

ORLANDO

What's here?
The paltry bottle that Darius quaff'd?

[He drinks, and she charms him with her wand, and he lies down to sleep.

Else would I set my mouth to Tigris' streams,
And drink up overflowing Euphrates.
My eyes are heavy, and I needs must sleep.

[**MELISSA** strikes with her wand, and the **SATYRS** enter with music, and play round about him; which done, they stay: he awakes and speaks.

What shows are these,
That fill mine eyes with view of such regard
As heaven admires to see my slumbering dreams!
Skies are fulfill'd with lamps of lasting joy,
That boast the pride of haught Latona's son,
Who lighteneth all the candles of the night.
Mnemosyne hath kiss'd the kingly Jove,
And entertain'd a feast within my brains,

Making her daughters solace on my brow.
Methinks, I feel how Cynthia tunes conceits
Of sad repent, and melloweth those desires
That frenzy scarce had ripen'd in my head.
Ate, I'll kiss thy restless cheek a while,
And suffer fruitless passion bide control.

[Lies down again.

MELISSA
O vos Silvani, Satyri, Faunique, deœque,
Nymphœ Hamadryades, Dryades, Parcœque potentes!
O vos qui colitis lacusque locosque profundos,
Infernasque domus et nigra palatia Ditis!
Tuque Demogorgon, qui noctis fata gubernas,
Qui regis infernum solium, cœlumque, solumque!
Exaudite preces, filiasque auferte micantes;
In caput Orlandi celestes spargite lymphas,
Spargite, quis misere revocetur rapta per umbras
Orlandi infelix anima

[Then let music play before him, and so go forth.

ORLANDO
What sights, what shapes, what strange-conceited dreams,
More dreadful than appear'd to Hecuba
When fall of Troy was figur'd in her sleep!
Juno, methought, sent down from heaven by Jove,
Came swiftly sweeping through the gloomy air;
And calling Iris, sent her straight abroad
To summon Fauns, the Satyrs, and the Nymphs,
The Dryades, and all the demigods,
To secret council; and, their parle past,
She gave them vials full of heavenly dew.
With that,
Mounted upon her parti-colour'd coach,
Being drawn with peacocks proudly through the air,
She flew with Iris to the sphere of Jove.
What fearful thoughts arise upon this show!
What desert grove is this? How thus disguis'd?
Where is Orgalio?

ORGALIO
Here, my lord.

ORLANDO
Sirrah, how came I thus disguis'd,
Like mad Orestes, quaintly thus attir'd?

ORGALIO
Like mad Orestes! nay, my lord, you may boldly justify the comparison, for Orestes was never so mad in his life as you were.

ORLANDO
What, was I mad? what Fury hath enchanted me?

MELISSA
A Fury, sure, worse than Megæra was,
That reft her son from trusty Pylades.

ORLANDO
Why, what art thou,
Some sibyl, or some goddess? freely speak.

MELISSA
Time not affords to tell each circumstance:
But thrice hath Cynthia chang'd her hue,
Since thou, infected with a lunacy,
Hast gadded up and down these lawnds and groves,
Performing strange and ruthful strategems,
All for the love of fair Angelica,
Whom thou with Medor didst suppose play'd false.
But Sacripant had graven these roundelays,
To sting thee with infecting jealousy:
The swain that told thee of their oft converse,
Was servant unto County Sacripant:
And trust me, Orlando, Angelica,
Though true to thee, is banish'd from the court,
And Sacripant
This day bids battle to Marsilius.
The armies ready are to give assail;
And on a hill that overpeers them both
Stand all the worthy matchless peers of France,
Who are in quest to seek Orlando out.
Muse not at this, for I have told thee true.
I am she that curèd thy disease.
Here take these weapons, given thee by the fates,
And hie thee, county, to the battle straight.

ORLANDO
Thanks, sacred goddess, for thy helping hand.
Thither will I hie to be reveng'd.

[Exeunt,

[Alarums: enter **SACRIPANT** crowned, and pursuing **MARSILIUS** and **MANDRICARD**.

SACRIPANT
Viceroys, you are dead;
For Sacripant, already crown'd a king,
Heaves up his sword to have your diadems.

MARSILIUS
Traitor, not dead, nor any whit dismay'd;
For dear we prize the smallest drop of blood.

[Enter **ORLANDO**, with a scarf before his face.

ORLANDO
Stay, princes,
'Base not yourselves, to combat such a dog.
Mount on your coursers, follow those that fly,
And let
Your conquering swords be tainted in their bloods:
Pass ye for him; he shall be combated.

[Exeunt **MARISILIUS** and **MANDRICARD**.

SACRIPANT
Why, what art thou that brav'st me thus?

ORLANDO
I am, thou see'st, a mercenary soldier,
Homely attir'd, but of so haughty thoughts,
As naught can serve to quench th' aspiring flames,
That burn as do the fires of Sicily,
Unless I win that princely diadem,
That seems so ill upon thy coward's head.

SACRIPANT
Coward!
To arms, sir boy! I will not brook these braves,
If Mars himself even from his fiery throne
Came arm'd with all his furnitures of war.

[They fight.

O villain! thou hast slain a prince.

ORLANDO
Then mayst thou think that Mars himself came down,
To vail thy plumes and heave thee from thy pomp.
Prove what thou art, I reck not of thy gree,
But I will have the conquest of my sword,

Which is the glory of thy diadem.

SACRIPANT
These words bewray thou art no base-born Moor,
But by descent sprung from some royal line:
Then freely tell me, what's thy name?

ORLANDO
Nay, first let me know thine.

SACRIPANT
Then know that thou hast slain Prince Sacripant.

ORLANDO
Sacripant!
Then let me at thy dying day entreat,
By that some sphere wherein thy soul shall rest,
If Jove deny not passage to thy ghost,
Thou tell me
Whether thou wrong'dst Angelica or no?

SACRIPANT
O, that's the sting that pricks my conscience!
O, that's the hell my thoughts abhor to think!
I tell thee, knight, for thou dost seem no less,
That I engrav'd the roundelays on the trees,
And hung the schedules of poor Medor's love,
Intending so to breed debate
Between Orlando and Angelica:
O, thus I wrong'd Orlando and Angelica!
Now tell me, what shall I call thy name?

ORLANDO
Then dead is the fatal author of my ill.
Base villain, vassal, unworthy of a crown,
Know that the man that struck the fatal stroke,
Is Orlando, the County Palatine,
Whom fortune sent to quittance all my wrongs.
Thou foil'd and slain, it now behoves me straight
To hie me fast to massacre thy men:
And so, farewell, thou devil in shape of man.

[Exit.

SACRIPANT
Hath Demogorgon, ruler of the fates,
Set such a baleful period on my life
As none might end the days of Sacripant

But mighty Orlando, rival of my love?
Now hold the fatal murderers of men
The sharpen'd knife ready to cut my thread,
Ending the scene of all my tragedy:
This day, this hour, this minute ends the days
Of him that liv'd worthy old Nestor's age.
Phœbus, put on thy sable-suited wreath,
Clad all thy spheres in dark and mourning weeds:
Parch'd be the earth, to drink up every spring:
Let corn and trees be blasted from above;
Heaven turn to brass, and earth to wedge of steel;
The world to cinders. Mars, come thundering down,
And never sheath thy swift-revenging sword,
Till, like the deluge in Deucalion's days,
The highest mountains swim in streams of blood.
Heaven, earth, men, beasts, and every living thing,
Consume and end with County Sacripant!

[Dies.

[Enter **MARSILIUS**, **MANDRICARD**, and the **TWELVE PEERS**, with **ANGELICA**.

MARSILIUS
Fought is the field, and Sacripant is slain,
With such a massacre of all his men,
As Mars, descending in his purple robe,
Vows with Bellona in whole heaps of blood
To banquet all the demigods of war.

MANDRICARD
See, where he lies slaughter'd without the camp,
And by a simple swain, a mercenary,
Who bravely took the combat to himself:
Might I but know the man that did the deed,
I would, my lord, etérnize him with fame.

OGIER
Leaving the factious county to his death,
Command, my lord, his body be convey'd
Unto some place, as likes your highness best.
See, Marsilius, posting through Africa,
We have found this straggling girl, Angelica,
Who, for she wrong'd her love Orlando,
Chiefest of the western peers, conversing
With so mean a man as Medor was,
We will have her punish'd by the laws of France,
To end her burning lust in flames of fire.

MARSILIUS
Beshrew you, lordings, but you do your worst;
Fire, famine, and as cruel death
As fell to Nero's mother in his rage.

ANGELICA
Father, if I may dare to call thee so,
And lords of France, come from the western seas,
In quest to find mighty Orlando out,
Yet, ere I die, let me have leave to say,
Angelica held ever in her thoughts
Most dear the love of County Palatine.
What wretch hath wrong'd us with suspect of lust,
I know not, I, nor can accuse the man;
But, by the heavens, whereto my soul shall fly,
Angelica did never wrong Orlando.
I speak not this as one that cares to live,
For why my thoughts are fully malcontent;
And I conjure you by your chivalry,
You quit Orlando's wrong upon Angelica.

[Enter **ORLANDO**, with a scarf before his face.

Oliver, Strumpet, fear not, for, by fair Maia's son,
This day thy soul shall vanish up in fire,
As Semele, when Juno wil'd the trull
To entertain the glory of her love.

ORLANDO
Frenchman, for so thy quaint arrayimports,
Be thou a peer, or be thou Charlemagne,
Or hadst thou Hector's or Achilles' heart,
Or never-daunted thoughts of Hercules,
That did in courage far surpass them all,
I tell thee, sir, thou liest in thy throat,—
The greatest brave Transalpine France can brook,—
In saying that sacred Angelica
Did offer wrong unto the Palatine.
I am a common mercenary soldier;
Yet, for I see my princess is abus'd
By new-come stragglers from a foreign coast,
I dare the proudest of these western lords
To crack a blade in trial of her right.

MANDRICARD
Why, foolish-hardy, daring, simple groom,
Follower of fond-conceited Phaëton,
Know'st thou to whom thou speak'st?

MARSILIUS
Brave soldier, for so much thy courage says,
These men are princes dipt within the blood
Of kings most royal, seated in the west,
Unfit to accept a challenge at your hand:
Yet thanks that thou wouldst in thy lord's defence
Fight for my daughter; but her guilt is known.

ANGELICA
Ay, rest thee, soldier, Angelica is false,—
False, for she hath no trial of her right:
Soldier, let me die for the 'miss of all.
Wert thou as stout as was proud Theseus,
In vain thy blade should offer my defence;
For why these be the champions of the world,
Twelve Peers of France that never yet were foil'd.

ORLANDO
How, madam, the Twelve Peers of France!
Why, let them be twelve devils of hell,
What I have said, thereto I'll pawn my sword,
To seal it on the shield of him that dares,
Malgrado of his honour, combat me.

OLIVER
Marry, sir, that dare I.

ORLANDO
You're a welcome man, sir.

TURPIN
Chastise the groom, Oliver, and learn him know
We are not like the boys of Africa.

ORLANDO
Hear you, sir?
You that so peremptorily bade him fight,
Prepare your weapons, for your turn is next:
'Tis not one champion can discourage me.
Come, are ye ready?

[He fights first with one, and these with the other, and overcomes them both.

So, stand aside:—
And, madam, if my fortune last it out,
I'll guard your person with Twelve Peers of France.

OGIER [Aside]
O Ogier, how canst thou stand, and see a slave
Disgrace the house of France?—Sirrah, prepare you;
For angry Nemesis sits on my sword
To be reveng'd.

ORLANDO
Well said, Frenchman! you have made a goodly oration: but you had
best to use your sword better, lest I beswinge you.

[They fight a good while, and then breathe.

OGIER
Howe'er disguis'd in base or Indian shape,
Ogier can well discern thee by thy blows;
For either thou art Orlando or the devil.

ORLANDO [Taking off his scarf]
Then, to assure you that I am no devil,
Here's your friend and companion, Orlando.

OGIER
And none can be more glad than Ogier is,
That he hath found his cousin in his sense.

OLIVER
Whenas I felt his blows upon my shield,
My teeth did chatter, and my thoughts conceiv'd,
Who might this be, if not the Palatine.

TURPIN
So had I said, but that report did tell
My lord was troubled with a lunacy.

ORLANDO
So was I, lordings; but give me leave awhile,
Humbly as Mars did to his paramour,
So to submit to fair Angelica.—
Pardon thy lord, fair saint Angelica,
Whose love, stealing by steps into extremes,
Grew by suspect to causeless lunacy.

ANGELICA
O no, my lord, but pardon my amiss;
For had not Orlando lov'd Angelica,
Ne'er had my lord fall'n into these extremes,
Which we will parley private to ourselves.
Ne'er was the queen of Cyprus half so glad

As is Angelica to see her lord,
Her dear Orlando, settled in his sense.

ORLANDO
Thanks, my sweet love.—
But why stand the Prince of Africa,
And Mandricard the King of Mexico,
So deep in dumps, when all rejoice beside?
First know, my lord, I slaughter'd Sacripant,
I am the man that did the slave to death;
Who frankly there did make confession,
That he engrav'd the roundelays on the trees,
And hung the schedules of poor Medor's love,
Intending by suspect to breed debate
Deeply 'twixt me and fair Angelica:
His hope had hap, but we had all the harm;
And now revenge leaping from out the seat
Of him that may command stern Nemesis,
Hath pour'd those treasons justly on his head.
What saith my gracious lord to this?

MARSILIUS
I stand amaz'd, deep over-drench'd with joy,
To hear and see this unexpected end:
So well I rest content.—Ye peers of France,
Sith it is prov'd Angelica is clear,
Her and my crown I freely will bestow
Upon Orlando, the County Palatine.

ORLANDO
Thanks, my good lord.—And now, my friends of France,
Frolic, be merry: we will hasten home,
So soon as King Marsilius will consent
To let his daughter wend with us to France.
Meanwhile we'll richly rig up all our fleet
More brave than was that gallant Grecian keel
That brought away the Colchian fleece of gold.
Our sails of sendal spread into the wind;
Our ropes and tacklings all of finest silk,
Fetch'd from the native looms of labouring worms,
The pride of Barbary, and the glorious wealth
That is transported by the western bounds;
Our stems cut out of gleaming ivory;
Our planks and sides fram'd out of cypress-wood,
That bears the name of Cyparissus' change,
To burst the billows of the ocean-sea,
Where Phœbus dips his amber tresses oft,
And kisses Thetis in the day's decline;

That Neptune proud shall call his Tritons forth
To cover all the ocean with a calm:
So rich shall be the rubbish of our barks,
Ta'en here for ballass to the ports of France,
That Charles himself shall wonder at the sight.
Thus, lordings, when our banquettings be done,
And Orlando espousèd to Angelica,
We'll furrow through the moving ocean,
And cheerly frolic with great Charlemagne.

[Exeunt **OMNES**.

Robert Greene - A Short Biography

Robert Greene was, by the best accounts available, born in Norwich in 1558 and baptised on July 11th.

As can be understood much of his early life was not recorded and few contemporary accounts exist to add to what we know. Greene is believed to have attended Norwich Grammar School but did attend Cambridge and received his in 1580, and an M.A. in 1583. He took no part, that we know of, in any of the Cambridge university dramatic productions. Academically he seemed to be nothing above fair. For his B.A. he graduated 38th out of the 41 students in his college, and 115th out of the total graduating class of 1580 of 205 students. For his M.A. it is believed, but not entirely proven, that he transferred to Clare College and was placed 5th out of the 12 students there, and 29th of the 129 students at the university graduating in that year.

But life was about to change. He moved to London and began an extraordinary chapter in his life and career as a widely published author. He was prolific, and of quality, publishing across many genres such as romances, plays and autobiography.

Greene's literary career began with the publication of the long romance, Mamillia, which was entered in the Stationers' Register on 3rd October 1580. Greene's romances were written in a highly wrought style which reached its peak in Pandosto (1588) and Menaphon (1589). Short poems and songs that he incorporated in some of the romances attest to his ability as a lyric poet. One song from Menaphon, 'Weep not my wanton, smile upon my knee, (a mother's lullaby to her baby son)', enjoyed immense success.

Within the space of a few years Greene had published over twenty-five works in prose across several genres and is regarded as 'England's first celebrity author'.

In 1588, he was granted an MA from Oxford University, almost certainly as a courtesy degree. Thereafter he sometimes placed the phrase 'Utruisq. Academiae in Artibus Magister', 'Master of Arts in both Universities' on the title page of his works.

As previously mentioned enough facts on Greene's life are not available so much is made of his autobiographical work 'The Repentance of Robert Greene', In it, Greene claimed to have travelled to

Italy and Spain; however, no evidence of Greene's continental trip has been found. Indeed, some scholars doubt that 'The Repentance of Robert Greene' was actually written by the man himself.

In another section of the book Greene claimed to have married a gentleman's daughter, whom he abandoned after having had a child by her and spent her dowry, after which she went to Lincolnshire, and he to London. In 'Four Letters and Certain Sonnets' (1592), Gabriel Harvey prints a letter allegedly written by Greene to his wife in which he addresses her as 'Doll'. However, research through the ages has failed to find any further evidence or record of this marriage. Perhaps it really is indeed a complete fiction and not even by him.

According to 'The Repentance of Robert Greene', Greene is alleged to have written 'A Groatsworth of Wit Bought with a Million of Repentance' during the month leading up to his death, including in it a letter to his wife asking her to forgive him and writing that he was sending their son back to her.

No record of facts survives to validate this. Again in 'Four Letters and Certain Sonnets', Gabriel Harvey claimed that Greene kept a mistress, Em, the sister of a criminal known as 'Cutting Ball' and later hanged at Tyburn. She is described as 'a sorry ragged quean of whom Greene had his base son Infortunatus Greene'.

The facts may be hidden but thankfully much of his work survives. He was perhaps one of the first English authors to support himself with his pen in an age when professional authorship was virtually unknown.

In his 'coney-catching' pamphlets, Greene portrays himself as a well-known public figure, narrating colourful inside stories of rakes and rascals duping young gentlemen and solid citizens out of their hard-earned money. These stories, told from the perspective of a repentant former rascal, have been considered autobiographical, and have been thought to incorporate many facts of Greene's own life thinly veiled as fiction: his early riotous living, his marriage and desertion of his wife and child for the sister of a notorious character of the London underworld, his dealings with players, and his success in the production of plays for them. However, the alternate account suggests that Greene invented almost everything, part of his undoubted skills of being a writer.

In addition to his prose works, Greene also wrote several plays, none of them published in his lifetime, including 'The Scottish History of James IV', 'Alphonsus', and his greatest popular success, 'Friar Bacon and Friar Bungay', as well as 'Orlando Furioso', based on Ludovico Ariosto's Orlando Furioso.

His plays earned himself the title as one of the 'University Wits', including George Peele, Thomas Nashe, and Christopher Marlowe.

As was common with the better talents of the time many works were latter attributed to their hand by unscrupulous printers and publishers eager to put a better name on the title page in their pursuit of sales. Greene has been proposed as the author of several dramas, including a second part to 'Friar Bacon' which may survive as 'John of Bordeaux', 'The Troublesome Reign of King John', 'George a Greene', 'Fair Em', 'A Knack to Know a Knave', 'Locrine', 'Selimus', and 'Edward III', and even Shakespeare's 'Titus Andronicus' and 'Henry VI' plays.

Greene is most familiar to Shakespeare scholars for his pamphlet Greene's 'Groats-Worth of Wit', which alludes to a line, "O tiger's heart wrapped in a woman's hide", found in Shakespeare's Henry VI, Part 3 (c. 1591–92):

'... for there is an upstart Crow, beautified with our feathers, that with his Tygers hart wrapt in a Players hyde, supposes he is as well able to bombast out a blanke verse as the best of you: and being an absolute Johannes fac totum, is in his owne conceit the onely Shake-scene in a countrey.'

Greene's complaint of an actor who states he can write as well as university-educated playwrights, alludes to the actor with a quote that appears in both the True Tragedy quarto and Shakespeare's Folio version of Henry VI, Part 3, and uses the term 'Shake-scene', a unique term never used before or after Greene's screed, to refer to the actor.

Robert Greene died 3rd September 1592, at the very young age of 34.

His death and burial were announced by Gabriel Harvey in a letter to Christopher Bird of Saffron Walden dated 5th September, first published as a 'butterfly pamphlet' about 8th September, and later expanded as 'Four Letters and Certain Sonnets', entered in the Stationers' Register on 4th December 1592.

However, no record of Greene's burial has ever been found.

Robert Greene – A Concise Bibliography

Prose works
Mamillia: A Mirror or Looking-glass for the Ladies of England (1583)
Mamillia: The Second Part of the Triumph of Pallas (1593)
The Anatomy of Lovers' Flatteries (1584)
The Myrrour of Modestie (1584)
Arbasto; The Anatomy of Fortune (1584)
Gwydonius; The Card of Fancy (1584)
The Debate Between Folly and Love (1584)
The Second Part of the Tritameron of Love (1587)
Planetomachia (1585)
An Oration or Funeral Sermon (1585)
Morando; The Tritameron of Love (1587)
Morando; The Second Part of the Tritameron of Love (1587)
Euphues: His Censure to Philautus (1587)
Greene's Farewell to Folly (1591)
Penelope's Web (c1587)
Alcida; Greene's Metamorphosis (1617)
Greenes Orpharion (1599)
Pandosto (1588)
Perimedes (1588)
Ciceronis Amor (1589)
Menaphon (1589)
The Spanish Masquerado (1589)

Greene's Mourning Garment (1590)
Greene's Never Too Late (1590)
Francesco's Fortunes, or The Second Part of Greene's Never Too Late (1590)
Greene's Vision, Written at the Instant of his Death (c1590)
The Royal Exchange (1590)
A Notable Discovery of Coosnage (1591)
The Second Part of Conycatching (1591)
The Black Books Messenger (1592)
A Disputation Between a Hee Conny-Catcher and a Shee Conny-Catcher (1592)
A Groatsworth of Wit Bought with a Million of Repentance (1592)
Philomela (1592)
A Quip for an Upstart Courtier (1592)
The Third and Last Part of Conycatching (1592)

Verse
A Maiden's Dream (1591)

Plays
Friar Bacon and Friar Bungay (circa 1590)
The History of Orlando Furioso (circa 1590)
A Looking Glass for London and England (with Thomas Lodge) (circa 1590)
The Scottish History of James the Fourth (circa 1590)
The Comical History of Alphonsus, King of Aragon (circa 1590)
Selimus (circa 1594)

www.ingramcontent.com/pod-product-compliance
Lightning Source LLC
Chambersburg PA
CBHW021943040426
42448CB00008B/1218